DEADLY LIZARD BITE!

by Meish Goldish

Consultant: Professor Bryan Grieg Fry
Head of Venom Evolution Laboratory
School of Biological Sciences
University of Queensland, Australia

BEARPORT
PUBLISHING

New York, New York

Credits

Cover, © Sergey Uryadnikov/Alamy, © Richard Susanto/Shutterstock, and © Ivona/Shutterstock; TOC, © Eric Isselee/Shutterstock; 4T, © Michael Turtle/Time Travel Turtle; 4B, © Joakimbkk/iStock; 4–5, © Gudkov Andrey/Shutterstock; 6L, © Eric Nathan/Alamy; 6–7, © Manfred Bail/imageBROKER/Alamy; 7R, © Michael Turtle/Time Travel Turtle; 9LT, © Kjersti Joergensen/Shutterstock; 9LB, © Sergey Uryadnikov/YAY Micro/AGE Fotostock; 9R, © AYImages/iStock; 10T, © Cyril Ruoso/Minden Pictures; 10B, © USO/iStock; 11, © M. Watson/Ardea/Mary Evans Picture Collection/AGE Fotostock; 12T, © Matthijs Kuijpers/Dreamstime; 12B, © Matthijs Kuijpers/Alamy; 13T, © Milan Zygmunt/Shutterstock; 13B, © Andrew DuBois/Alamy; 14T, © Jared Hobbs/All Canada Photos/AGE Fotostock; 14B, © Daniel Heuclin/NPL/Minden Pictures; 15, © Daniel Heuclin/Nature Production/Minden Pictures; 16, © jhayes44/iStock; 17T, © Matthijs Kuijpers/Dreamstime; 17B, © irin717/iStock; 18, © Mikhail Blajenov/Dreamstime; 19, © Michael D. Kern/NPL/Minden Pictures; 20L, © John Cancalosi/Mary Evans Picture Library Ltd./AGE Fotostock; 20R, © Thomas Wiewandt/Wild Horizons; 21, © Humble Bee Films; 22 (L to R), © Sergey Uryadnikov/Shutterstock, © Kris Wiktor/Shutterstock, and © reptiles4all/Shutterstock.

Publisher: Kenn Goin
Senior Editor: Joyce Tavolacci
Creative Director: Spencer Brinker
Photo Researcher: Thomas Persano

Library of Congress Cataloging-in-Publication Data

Names: Goldish, Meish, author.
Title: Deadly lizard bite! / by Meish Goldish ; consultant, Professor Bryan
   Grieg Fry, Head of Venom Evolution Laboratory, School of Biological
   Sciences, University of Queensland, Australia.
Description: New York, New York : Bearport Publishing, [2019] | Series:
   Envenomators | Includes bibliographical references
   and index.
Identifiers: LCCN 2018010874 (print) | LCCN 2018012095 (ebook) |
   ISBN 9781684027033 (ebook) | ISBN 9781684026579 (library)
Subjects: LCSH: Lizards—Juvenile literature. | Lizards—Venom—Juvenile
   literature. | Poisonous animals—Juvenile literature.
Classification: LCC QL666.L2 (ebook) | LCC QL666.L2 G65 2019 (print) |
   DDC 597.95—dc23
LC record available at https://lccn.loc.gov/2018010874

For more information, write to Bearport Publishing Company, Inc., 45 West 21st Street, Suite 3B, New York, New York 10010. Printed in the United States of America.

10 9 8 7 6 5 4 3 2 1

Contents

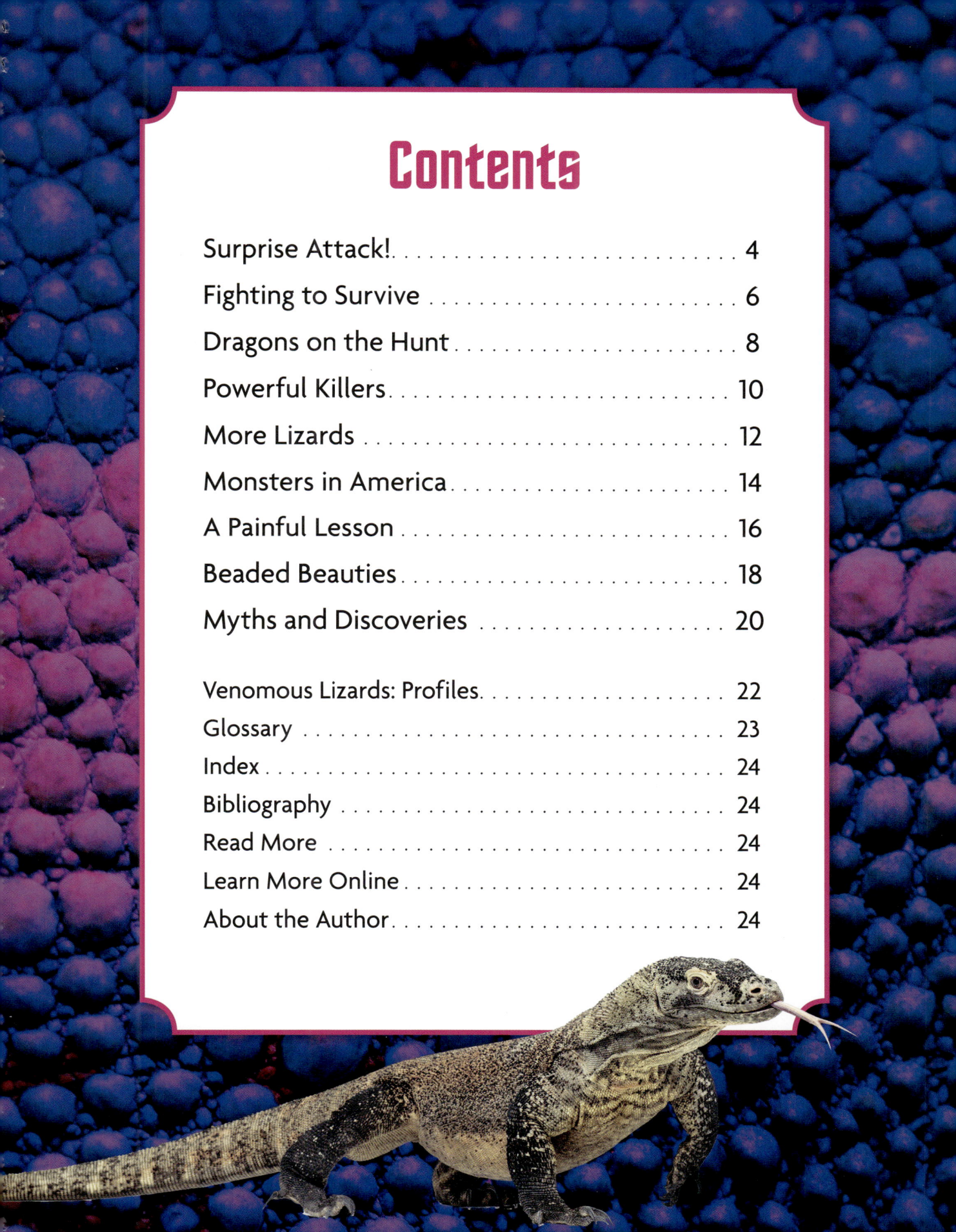

Surprise Attack!

One morning in 2009, a guide named Maen at Komodo National Park in Indonesia sat at his office desk. Suddenly, he felt something move near his feet. When he looked down, he couldn't believe his eyes. "I saw a Komodo dragon under this table," Maen said. The huge lizard was staring up at him. Maen slowly drew back his legs from the **venomous** creature.

Komodo dragons are the largest lizards in the world. They can grow up to 10 feet (3 m) long and weigh more than 300 pounds (136 kg)!

Maen at his desk

Komodo National Park is home to over 5,000 Komodo dragons.

In an instant, the animal **lunged** at Maen. It sank its sharp teeth into his foot, ripping through his flesh. Crying out in pain, Maen used his other foot to pin down the Komodo's neck. Then, with his bare hands, he pulled open the lizard's mouth and freed his injured foot. The Komodo's razor-sharp teeth sliced his right hand. Blood splattered everywhere. Would Maen escape with his life?

The Komodo dragon had wandered into Maen's office after a cleaning person accidentally left a door open. The lizard had probably smelled food inside.

Fighting to Survive

Badly injured, Maen shouted for help. Park workers raced to save him. Unfortunately, the blood on the floor attracted other Komodo dragons. "There were about seven dragons, all bigger," Maen recalled. A worker used a large stick to fight off the venomous dragons, while other rescuers carried Maen outside.

Workers at Komodo National Park use long sticks to protect themselves from the large lizards.

Komodo dragons have a great sense of smell. They can sniff out fresh blood from as far away as 5 miles (8 km).

Maen was then flown to a hospital where he underwent six hours of lifesaving **surgery**. It took 55 stitches to close his bite wounds. After six months, he returned to work. Maen considers himself lucky. "I thought I wouldn't survive," he said. "If the Komodo had had a bigger neck, I couldn't have held its mouth open."

Maen's foot and hand (right) healed after many months. Despite his terrifying experience, he still works at the park. He doesn't blame the lizard for attacking.

Dragons on the Hunt

Komodo dragons live only on five islands in Indonesia. The huge lizards range in color from black to yellow-gray and have thick, rough skin. They eat whichever animals they can find—both large and small. Deer is their favorite **prey**. However, they also eat wild pigs, water buffalo, and even younger Komodo dragons.

Where Komodo Dragons Live

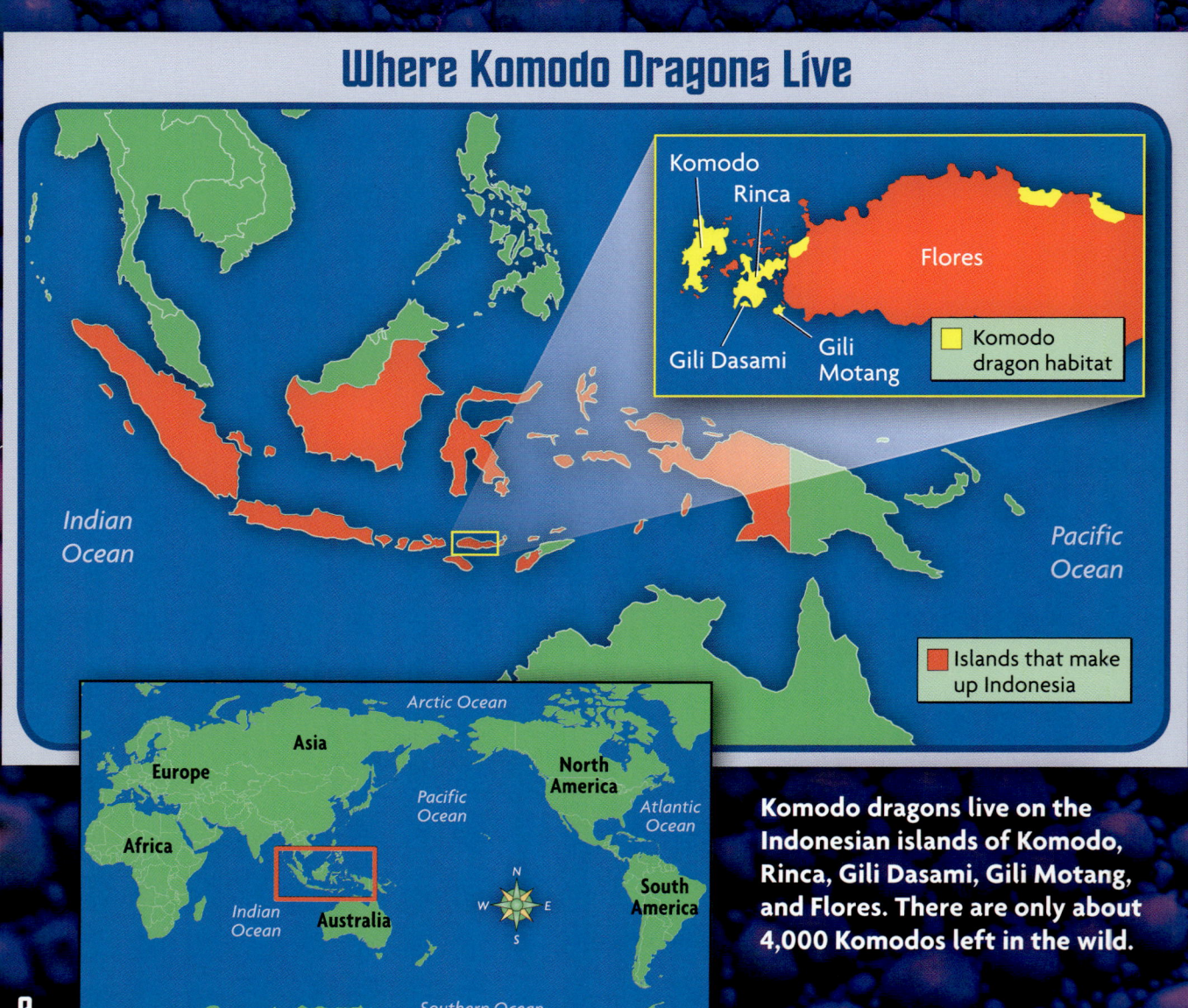

Komodo

Rinca

Flores

Gili Dasami

Gili Motang

Komodo dragon habitat

Indian Ocean

Pacific Ocean

Islands that make up Indonesia

Arctic Ocean

Asia

Europe

North America

Pacific Ocean

Atlantic Ocean

Africa

Indian Ocean

Australia

South America

Antarctica

Southern Ocean

N
W   E
S

Komodo dragons live on the Indonesian islands of Komodo, Rinca, Gili Dasami, Gili Motang, and Flores. There are only about 4,000 Komodos left in the wild.

How does a Komodo find prey? It flicks its long, forked tongue in and out. This helps it pick up the smell of any animals in the area. Once the Komodo senses food, it may chase after the animal or wait for it to come closer. Then, using its strong, curved claws, the giant lizard grabs its victim. Yet how do Komodos kill large animals, such as deer or water buffalo?

Timor deer

Water buffalo

A Komodo dragon is a type of monitor lizard. This group includes about 80 species.

How did the Komodo dragon get its name? Its long, scaly body and forked tongue reminded people of fire-breathing dragons from storybooks.

9

Powerful Killers

A Komodo dragon overpowers large prey with three weapons: strong muscles, sharp teeth, and venom. The Komodo sinks its **serrated** teeth into the victim's neck. The teeth are so sharp that they cut right to the bone. Then the lizard uses its leg and neck muscles to grab and hold on to the animal. When the dragon bites, venom from a **gland** in its lower jaw is pushed deeply into the victim's bite wound.

Razor-sharp teeth

A Komodo dragon bites a goat. The lizard uses its teeth, muscle power, and venom to kill its prey.

Komodo venom stops blood from **clotting**, so the bite victim bleeds heavily. It soon grows weak and dies. Around 70 percent of deer die from blood loss within 30 minutes of a Komodo bite. The giant lizard uses its sharp claws and teeth to rip apart the softest parts of its prey's body, such as the belly. Then, it tears off large chunks of meat and swallows them whole. A Komodo dragon can **consume** 80 percent of its body weight in a single meal!

A Komodo dragon can swallow a piece of food that's larger than its own head.

Komodo dragon venom contains more than 600 different **toxins**!

More Lizards

Not all lizards are as deadly as the Komodo dragon. In fact, most lizards do not produce any venom. Of the 4,000 types of lizards that exist, only a few kinds are known to carry venom. These include other monitor lizards and the rare tree-dwelling alligator lizard.

Lizards are part of a larger group of animals called reptiles. All lizards have a long body and tail, and tough skin covered with scales.

Blue-tailed monitor lizard

Arboreal alligator lizard

Two other well-known venomous lizards are Gila (HEE-luh) monsters and Mexican beaded lizards. Like Komodos, both have venom glands in their lower jaws. Their bites are painful but not as **lethal** as those of Komodo dragons because they contain less venom and **inflict** smaller wounds. The venom from a Gila monster or a Mexican beaded lizard can still kill an animal. However, neither lizard can take down large prey.

Gila monster

There may be many more venomous lizards yet to be discovered.

Mexican beaded lizard

Monsters in America

Gila monsters live in the deserts of the southwestern United States and northwestern Mexico. They have round black and yellow or pink scales called osteoderms. Gilas are much smaller than Komodos—only about the size of a small cat. However, they're the largest lizards in the United States.

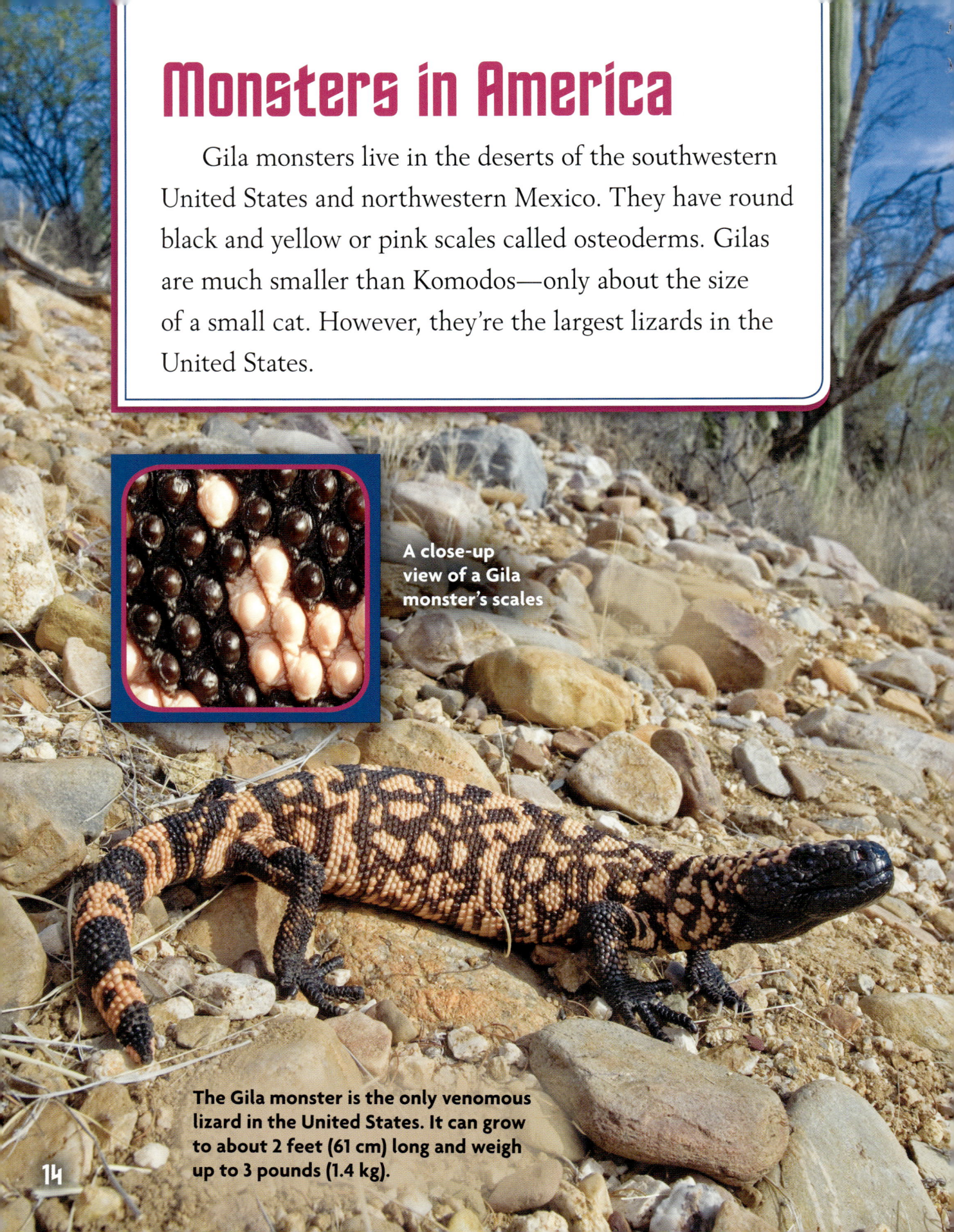

A close-up view of a Gila monster's scales

The Gila monster is the only venomous lizard in the United States. It can grow to about 2 feet (61 cm) long and weigh up to 3 pounds (1.4 kg).

Gila monsters spend much of the day underground. At night, when it's cooler, they come out to hunt. They eat mostly baby **mammals**, birds, and eggs. When a Gila finds a meal, it chomps down on its victim with its strong jaws. Sometimes, it holds on for as long as 15 minutes! Small grooves in the lizard's teeth help the venom to seep into the victim.

The Gila might also chew its victim's flesh to help spread the venom deeper into the wound.

A Gila monster eating a bird's egg

Where Gila Monsters Live

Nevada
Utah
Colorado
California
Arizona
New Mexico
Gila River
Pacific Ocean
MEXICO

Gila monsters are found in parts of Arizona, California, Nevada, Utah, and New Mexico. They also live in Mexico. They were named after the Gila River in Arizona, where they were first found.

☐ Gila monster habitat

CANADA
UNITED STATES
MEXICO

A Painful Lesson

Gila monsters will only attack people if they feel threatened. In 2008, a visitor at Arizona's Saguaro National Park learned this lesson the hard way. The 24-year-old caught a wild Gila and placed it on his shoulders. He thought the animal looked friendly and harmless.

Saguaro National Park

Chomp! The frightened Gila bit the man on the neck. The lizard's venom seeped into the wound. The man tried to remove the lizard, but it bit him again on the hand. Soon, the venom took effect. The man had trouble breathing and began to throw up. Park rangers rushed him to a nearby hospital. Luckily, the man soon recovered.

A Gila monster's venom is as strong as that of a rattlesnake's. However, the Gila injects less venom than the snake, so its bite is not as harmful to humans.

Never pick up wild animals. It's best to keep a safe distance from them.

The last reported death from a Gila monster bite was in 1939.

Beaded Beauties

A close cousin to the Gila monster is the Mexican beaded lizard. It's called *beaded* because, similar to the Gila, it's covered with scales that look like beads. Mexican beaded lizards are larger than Gila monsters and can grow over 3 feet (91 cm) long.

Mexican beaded lizard

Mexican beaded lizards live in deserts, forests, and grassy areas of western Mexico and Central America.

Where Mexican Beaded Lizards Live

UNITED STATES

MEXICO

Gulf of Mexico

BELIZE

Pacific Ocean

GUATEMALA

EL SALVADOR

HONDURAS

N
W   E
S

Mexican beaded lizard habitat

UNITED STATES

MEXICO

CENTRAL AMERICA

Mexican beaded lizards spend most of their time underground or beneath rocks. Their dark color helps them blend into their surroundings. At night, they come out to hunt rabbits, mice, frogs, and other small animals. Like Gila monsters, they bite their prey and spread venom in their victim's flesh as they chew.

Mexican beaded lizards hunt mostly on the ground. However, they sometimes climb a tree to find their next meal.

Few animals hunt Mexican beaded lizards and Gila monsters. The lizards' colored scales scare away most attackers. If threatened, the lizards also make a hissing sound.

Myths and Discoveries

Every year, scientists learn more and more about venomous lizards. Sometimes, their findings **disprove** earlier beliefs. For example, in the late 1800s, scientists thought that Gila monsters killed their prey because of their bad breath, not because of their venom. Others falsely believed that when a Gila bit its victim, the lizard wouldn't let go until the sun went down.

In the 1800s, American settlers heard tall tales about wild Gila monsters' attacking and killing people in the Southwest.

A scientist collects a Gila monster's venom.

Today, venom from Gila monsters is being used to make a drug to treat people with **type 2 diabetes**. The drug has been nicknamed "lizard spit."

Until 2009, many scientists didn't think that Komodo dragons were venomous. They believed that **bacteria** in the Komodo's mouth **infected** and killed bite victims. In 2005, Australian researcher Bryan Fry discovered that Komodos make deadly venom, which many people now believe is what ultimately kills the lizards' victims. There's no telling what future research will uncover about these fascinating creatures!

Professor Bryan Fry studies Komodo dragons and other venomous animals up close. He suspects that iguanas may also produce venom.

Venomous Lizards
—PROFILES—

	Gila Monster	Komodo Dragon	Mexican Beaded Lizard

DESCRIPTION	Gila monsters have stout bodies with broad heads and stumpy tails. They are mostly black with beaded scales, which vary in color from yellow to orange.	Komodo dragons are the largest, heaviest lizards in the world. They have long tails, strong necks, and sturdy limbs. Adult dragons are black to yellowish gray with distinct, large scales.	The Mexican beaded lizard has a thick, fleshy tail that is slightly shorter than the rest of its body, and short powerful limbs. The reptile is mostly black with white or yellow spots and is covered with beadlike scales.
SIZE	Up to 24 inches (61 cm) long Up to 3 pounds (1.4 kg)	Up to 10 feet (3 m) long Up to 300 pounds (136 kg)	Up to 36 inches (91 cm) long Up to 6 pounds (2.7 kg)
VENOM and Its Effects	The Gila's venom has toxins that can cause bleeding, breathing difficulty, bulging of the eyes, **lethargy**, and partial **paralysis**.	The Komodo's venom has toxins that can cause excessive bleeding and shock, prevent blood from clotting, and lower blood pressure.	The Mexican beaded lizard's venom has toxins that can cause extreme pain, bleeding, swelling, a drop in blood pressure, breathing difficulty, and heart problems.

Glossary

bacteria (bak-TIHR-ee-uh) tiny living things that can cause disease

clotting (KLOT-ing) becoming thicker and ceasing to flow

consume (kuhn-SOOM) to eat or drink something

disprove (diss-PROOV) to show that something is not true

gland (GLAND) a body part that produces natural chemicals, such as venom

infected (in-FEK-tid) filled with harmful germs

inflict (in-FLIKT) to cause something painful or unpleasant

lethal (LEE-thuhl) able to kill

lethargy (LETH-er-jee) the state of being drowsy or not energetic

lunged (LUHNJD) moved forward quickly and without warning

mammals (MAM-uhlz) warm-blooded animals that have hair or fur and drink their mother's milk

paralysis (puh-RAL-uh-siss) the inability to move or feel a part of one's body

prey (PRAY) an animal that's hunted down and attacked or eaten by another animal

serrated (ser-AY-tid) having teeth like a saw or a knife

surgery (SUHR-juhr-ee) an operation that treats injuries or diseases by fixing or removing body parts

toxins (TOKS-inz) poisonous substances

type 2 diabetes (TIPE TOO dye-uh-BEE-teez) a disease in which people have too much sugar in their blood

venomous (VEHN-uhm-uss) capable of making a toxin-filled fluid called venom

Index

Bibliography

Fry, Bryan. *Venomous Reptiles and Their Toxins: Evolution, Pathophysiology and Biodiscovery.* New York: Oxford (2015).

Wilcox, Christie. *Venomous: How Earth's Deadliest Creatures Mastered Biochemistry.* New York: Scientific American (2016).

Read More

Lunis, Natalie. *Komodo Dragon: The World's Biggest Lizard (Super-Sized!).* New York: Bearport (2007).

Phillips, Dee. *Gila Monster's Burrow (The Hole Truth! Underground Animal Life).* New York: Bearport (2015).

Learn More Online

To learn more about venomous lizards, visit
www.bearportpublishing.com/Envenomators

About the Author

Meish Goldish has written more than 300 books for children. He lives in Brooklyn, New York.